The Elixir of Enlightenment

179 Church
NJ, N.

The
Elixir of
Enlightenment

A.H. Almaas

SAMUEL WEISER, INC.
York Beach, Maine

First published in 1984 by
Samuel Weiser, Inc.
P.O. Box 612
York Beach, Maine 03910-0612

Third printing, 1996

Library of Congress Card Catalog Number: 84-50159

ISBN 8-87728-613-2
CCP

Typeset in 11 point Garamond

Printed in the United States of America

The paper used in this publication meets the minimum require-
ments of the American National Standard for Permanence of
Paper for Printed Library Materials Z39.48-1984.

CONTENTS

EDITOR'S PREFACE

The "elixir" of which the title speaks is *essence*, the presence or substance which inspires and enables us to move toward "enlightenment."

Those who attempt to address the problem of their own and others' human suffering often confront barriers or impasses which are difficult to understand. This book explores and explains some of those barriers. It reveals how a precise understanding of the personality of the seeker can free a person's inner resources so that the essential being itself, in harmony with, rather than opposed to, the personal life, can move us toward understanding.

In addition, the author illuminates the reasons for the frequent failure of the various teachings to reach the "ordinary" person: as long as the material, emotional, mental and social realities which most of us identify with are rejected, rather than accepted and understood, we will not see the teachings as relevant to our lives.

The understanding communicated in this book is part of a larger context: the author is the teacher of a school, described at the end of this volume, within which has arisen a synthesis of modern psychological knowledge and methods with ancient spiritual wisdom and techniques. But the relevance of this work is not limited to those who share this particular context. Any person who has been intrigued by, and yet ultimately frustrated with, the spiritual and psychological approaches to the issue of human suffering which abound in the current Western world, will find value in this analysis of the reasons for the limited effectiveness of these teachings, and in the unusual view presented here of the relationship between personality and true Being.

Alia Johnson
Berkeley, October, 1983

The Elixir of Enlightenment

CHAPTER ONE
THE SITUATION

Hum... predicament
We suffer

 curious predicament faces human beings—a dilemma which is a predicament we usually consider part of being human, part of what characterizes humanity, and is the intimate personal experience of almost every individual.

This predicament is the paradoxical situation of every person: that we desire happiness, freedom, and release, and yet continue to suffer—physically, emotionally, mentally and spiritually. We want happiness; we want release from our suffering and anguish. We are always seeking liberation from emotional and mental bondage, but we continue to suffer. Meaningless suffering abounds everywhere. In fact, it keeps accumulating. Even when our pain is diminished, the relief is small and transitory. Some people manage to accept suffering to some degree. This helps, but does not resolve the predicament.

Happiness keeps eluding us. Suffering and running from suffering are the permanent central preoccupation of the majority of people. In every person there lies buried deep in the heart, perhaps only faintly experienced, a desire for a certain sort of life: a life that is desired at the depth of man's heart, a life that is free and unencumbered, a life that is full of beauty, joy and fulfillment. But this life remains a dream, an inaccessable and distant ideal. When we feel joy, fulfillment and beauty, these experiences usually pass through us briefly, and leave behind them a deep longing and a sense of lack. Permanent and abiding fulfillment, a life of continuing beauty and expanding freedom, is rarely realized.

Our longing for the fulfilled life is increased by the fact that throughout the centuries, there have always been a few individuals who have made the ideal into a beautiful and living reality for themselves, and by the example of their own lives, have shown that it is possible, it is attainable.

Most spiritual teachers and spiritual movements have this ideal as their aim. Liberation and fulfillment are seen as the goal of inner work, whether they be psychological, spiritual, or essential. Throughout history, realized men have given humanity this hope, that liberation is possible and attainable. Buddha, for instance, emphasized enlightenment as the solution to man's suffering, and Christ taught freedom through truth and love. Many others have contributed to this hope, men who freed themselves and sought, out of compassion and love, to guide their fellow humans in their search for release from suffering.

Since the beginning of man's experience as a separate ego, and his resulting alienation from his true being, there have been teachers and religions whose purpose was to help people maintain a connection with or return to the essential Being. And in recent times, various kinds of psychologies and psychotherapies have been formulated to help alleviate man's most severe inner sufferings.

Many of us have benefited from these efforts, have felt our suffering decrease, and even found some peace and fulfillment. And humanity as a whole has benefited. However, this predicament—that man wishes to be free from suffering and yet continues to suffer—is very much present in the lives of all but a few unique

In spite of vast amt. of
Suff, only few people are
attracted to spot + study
the eff / end

individuals. Suffering abounds and is still the primary experience and the day-to-day reality of most people.

The existence of teachings about enlightenment, liberation, realization, fulfillment and the like make the situation even more curious. We find that very few individuals actually respond to these teachings. Many people are aware of their presence and their promise; still, only a few respond, and fewer still embark on the various paths. Many hear or read about the teachings; many believe in them, and see much truth in them, but few actually respond in terms of taking any action.

Teachers and religious leaders will explain this by saying that the people who don't respond are being blinded and held back by their greed, selfishness, attachments, fear, worldly concerns or desires, egotism, ignorance, and so on.

This is obviously true, but does not say anything useful. This attitude of blaming the student for the very thing which causes his suffering does not lead to any useful change. Why has there been no significant advance in solving this impasse? A teaching is useful only if it can reach people, only if it can reach them in a way that will enable them to respond effectively. To put the blame on the people themselves, to say they are ignorant and egoistic does not help, and the aim of a teaching is to help, not to explain or blame. A teaching is useful if it can help the individual attain liberation, but this is irrelevant if the individual does not take the initial steps toward liberation.

So, much of the message of the teachings has been seen as irrelevant or actively discouraging to most people. There seems to be little connection between the actual problems of one's life and the religious and spiritual teachings one encounters. There is, for example, the common idea that only those who *leave* their worldly problems, and become monks, nuns, yogis or saints, can attain a deep knowledge of true Being. So for most of human history, these teachings have failed to reach the common person.

The question of the strange failure of spiritual teachings to make possible actual liberation gets even more curious if we shift our attention to those who actually respond to a teaching and enter a path. Here the mystery deepens. We find that the great majority of these individuals do not attain realization. Those who do find freedom from their suffering by following one spiritual path or another are very few, a meager minority.

Some may certainly find a measure of peace, fulfillment or a degree of freedom. But this definitely falls short of their aim, and of what is possible. Isn't it curious that the sincerity of their efforts and the longing of their whole being, cannot accomplish what they wish?

Why is this? How can this be? Why is it that only a few attain the promise, only a few achieve a life of genuine fulfillment? The teachers of the various paths explain: Those people who fail are hampered by their egoism; they could not surrender their selfishness; their attachments interfered with their intentions.

And certainly this is true. But just as it is true that it is the student's responsibility to surrender attachments, to face his fear, his greed, his selfishness and go beyond these, it is the responsibility of the teacher to be accurate and effective in his communication with his student, and to use extraordinary skill and understanding.

We are interested in understanding why so few achieve the freedom they seek. Perhaps we can find some neglected gaps in the teachings, in their methods or their formulations, or in the way these are communicated. This may give us clues in dealing with this dilemma.

So we continue to ask: Why is it that the teachings do not work, except in a few isolated instances? Why is it that all these wonderful teachings and these various powerful methods touch only a few, a few of the many who actually practice these teachings? A realized teacher might have thousands of students but it is rare if even a handful of them actually attain liberation.

It is usually asserted then, as we have pointed out, that the student has failed, that his dedication or surrender was not complete or deep enough. This is true. But the responsibility does not end there. For it is also true that the teacher has failed: the teacher has not been able to penetrate the student's mind and heart. The inner endeavor is a conjoint one. Both teacher and student work together. When the endeavor fails the two of them have failed. And so has the teaching.

The student has, so far, borne the brunt of the blame for the failure. But we are saying here that there are more factors involved, and they are all responsible for the failure: the student, the teacher, the teaching and the methods. It is not a question of who or what is at fault. Useful understanding is what we need here.

It might be absolutely true that the student has not surrendered himself to the teaching, is not dedicated enough to the practice, is too identified with his ego or personality. But here it is valid to ask: Can anything be done in such a situation? Is it possible to communicate to such a student in a way that will penetrate his resistance, in a manner that will work for the liberation he wishes? Is there a truly effective method that will make the endeavor successful, or more successful?

In considering these questions, we are faced with the unchallenged belief that attaining liberation is so difficult that it is normal that so few manage to do it. Many teachers have asserted that achieving liberation and fulfillment is the most difficult task there is.

But we ask: Is it really the nature of this endeavor that it be so difficult and nearly impossible to complete? Is it the nature of the endeavor, or could it be that our understanding is not developed enough to make the achievement of liberation more within reach? And, aside from the question of complete liberation, is it possible for a greater number of people to arrive at a partial liberation, where their lives are governed by truth, love and joy?

Is it possible that there are gaps in our understanding? Is it possible that there is a specific kind of understanding that is not yet available? Is it possible that we are not yet applying some understanding that already exists?

If we believe that all the difficulty lies within the nature of the endeavor itself, then not much can be done and the situation is quite hopeless. But if that is not the case, if some of the difficulty or even a large part of it is due to other factors, then what are those factors and what exactly can be done?

It is our view that although the difficulty does lie somewhat in the nature of the task, it is also due to other factors—and these other factors can be recognized, isolated and dealt with. This will bring about a certain understanding that will lead to ways of dealing more effectively with the dilemma.

In the next chapter we will discuss some of the general factors we see contributing to the present situation in a way that will point to some solution. Then, in the final chapter we will discuss again, in a general way, some possible solutions for the predicament of human suffering, at least solutions for some of the factors contributing to this situation.

CHAPTER TWO
THE PROBLEM

Our attempt to elucidate some of the factors contributing to man's dilemma is in the spirit of support and enhancement of the already existing knowledge and understanding about the solutions to man's suffering. The paths to man's liberation have been known since ancient times. They have been formulated in various ways depending on the era and on the teacher.

We are not offering fundamentally new solutions here. Nor are we opposing the already existing solutions or the already existing teachings. The major teachings, like those of Buddha, Christ and Mohammed, are timeless and universal, and have done much to serve mankind. Our attempt is to bring to light some of the considerations that hinder both teacher and student. We want to point out some of the factors that are ignored, not acknowledged or not taken into account in most circumstances. We want to understand first why so few people in the world respond to the already existing teachings, and then why most of the disciples of any teaching do not actually accomplish the task. We want especially to investigate, as much as we are able to, what does make a given teaching effective in isolated cases but not in the vast majority of others.

We will not go into much detail about the factors already known and generally accepted, such as the influence of the environment, society, the economy, childhood conditioning, and the paucity of real teachers. Our concern with causes already mentioned—such as the part played by egoism, selfishness, attachment, ignorance and desire—will be to discuss them from a different point of view.

It is interesting to note that these causes not only account for our failure to relieve our suffering, but also account for the suffering itself. The existence of suffering, the lack of freedom and contentment, is seen as caused by ignorance, selfishness, greed, attachment and the like. These factors are, in fact, an explanation of the lack of enlightenment and fulfillment. And solutions found usually involve elimination of these factors.

Although these factors explain also the difficulty of pursuing spiritual paths, simply explaining the difficulty does not allow us to eliminate it.

Let us for a moment turn our attention to one of the commonly known factors contributing to man's suffering: desire. Many teachings have stressed that if man indulges in fulfilling his usual desires, this will contribute to his suffering, and, more particularly, will make it difficult for him to traverse any path of liberation. Desire for pleasure, for love, for security, for anything, is seen as a major barrier to realization. Most religions and most teachers have given this message to humanity.

But the response to this message is minimal. People might admire and love a teaching, but do not usually respond to this insight about desire. Some might, out of devotion to a teaching or teacher, genuinely believe this understanding about desire, but they still would not respond to it, nor act according to their belief. In fact, frequently, they would not even try to follow this teaching.

Most bsliv this truth where
dos is uf mind rests the heart &
body

Let us look at the majority of Buddhist students, for example. They believe in the truth of Buddha's teaching about desire. But it does not really touch them, or their lives, in a way that will lead to their emancipation. Only a few will completely respond to it.

This is very curious. The understanding is accurate. Desire is actually one of the main roots of suffering. This has been seen by all realized beings. The students believe this understanding, have faith in their teachers, love the Buddha and his teaching. However, they do not actually live their lives according to this truth—not in any significant way.

Again, this is curious. In fact, this is the same dilemma we have discussed in Chapter One. But now we see it in a more specific and concrete way, and maybe this narrowing down of the focus will help us in our understanding. Let us look more closely at the situation. The student believes that desire is the root of suffering as the Buddha, and his teacher or guru have told him. But does he really believe it? If he does, he believes with his mind, with his intellect. But his heart does not completely believe, neither does his body. Although he says he believes, and might understand on some level that desire is the root of suffering, he continues desiring pleasure, love, recognition, security, material possessions, fame and so on. And more than that, he strongly believes in the rightness of this desiring. He does not question these desires at a deep level. His life is constructed of them, in all ways shaped by them. More than anything else, he believes in his desires, especially in the depths of his unconscious. And so, at this deepest level, he does not believe in the Buddha's teachings, regardless of how much he loves and respects the teaching and wants to adhere to it.

And because at this deep level he does not believe in the teachings and unconsciously actually rejects it, he cannot be touched by it and he cannot follow the teaching in his life, or finds it difficult to follow because in the deepest part of his unconscious he cannot relate to it. If he really looks at his experience, he will not find any reason why he should believe it. He has not experienced the truth that desire is the root of suffering. Believing the teaching does not make it a knowing for him. He cannot believe deeply because he has no experiential knowledge that desire causes pain. He may see

Continue to p v13 re cign objits
uf belief if all the gods & will be
happy Never really quest why they
the grow

that the pursuit of certain of his desires, for material possessions or relationships or status, for example, are connected with his suffering. He may even see that even when some of his desires are gratified, he continues to suffer. A new car brings only a temporary pride, a new job a brief rise in self-esteem. But whatever new desires arise to replace the old ones, including the desire to end his suffering by becoming "enlightened," entail precisely the same suffering as did the original "naive" ones.

A student's belief in the teaching regarding desire is undermined by the deeper unbelief and rejection of the teaching, and he rejects the teaching because he believes himself. He believes his experience. His teacher can see very clearly that the student's trouble is due to his desires, but he cannot see that himself.

So the student is not touched by the teaching, because, according to his personal experience which relies on, and has always relied on desire, it is not true. The teaching is true for Buddha, but not for him. It is true, in an ultimate way for him, but he doesn't know that. In fact, the teaching contradicts his basic beliefs and all his understanding of his experience. At the depths of his personality, he believes he will get whatever he wants or needs by desiring it enough, and that he cannot have what he wants unless he desires it. In fact, at the very depths of his unconscious he feels and believes that he will not survive physically if he does not pursue his desires. All realized people attain their realization by seeing for themselves that they actually believed in their desires for their very physical survival. The average person believes this also, but he does not know he believes it. This belief, nonetheless, runs his life to an extent that very few people are aware of.

The Noble Truth that desire is at the root of suffering is such a deep truth that it is not easy to see experientially, except after long inner work. It is naive to imagine that the student will be convinced of this deep universal truth just by looking at his everyday desires and by noticing the frustration that arises. When an individual suffers due to desire, he usually attributes the suffering to the lack or loss of gratification, and not to the desiring itself. This means he believes desire is fine if gratification is forthcoming, if he gets what he wants.

But this is not Buddha's teaching about desire. The issue is not the possibility of no gratification. The teaching is very clear that the movement of desire itself is suffering. But this perception is very subtle. It cannot be understood except at very fine levels of consciousness. In fact, the complete conviction about the teaching regarding desire does not come about until the later stages of the path, when the individual can see and feel for himself that the teaching is indeed true.

For the average student, the situation is very difficult. The student not only rejects the teaching, in a deep, unconscious way, but in addition, he cannot see how this teaching is relevant to him or to his life. His everyday concerns have nothing to do, as far as he can see, with the question of desire or no desire. His everyday preoccupations, where his attention and interest lie, are not on a level where the question of desire is relevant. Maybe he is concerned with certain difficult life situations, and his real interest is in learning how to deal with them. Maybe he is concerned with some emotional conflicts that need first to be resolved in order to even have the energy to think about desires. Maybe he is primarily concerned with issues of self-image that are difficult for him to disengage from.

Of course, at the root of these concerns lies the issue of desire, but his awareness cannot go to that depth. He will have to deal with his own concerns first, one way or another. To expect him to see all his preoccupations from the perspective of the issue of desire is unrealistic.

We see, from all of this, that although the teaching regarding desire is accurate and of great value, it is not relevant for the average student. It is not relevant because he is not able to relate to it in any real way. The teaching, as it is stated and propagated, is not appropriate to him, to his life and to his state of consciousness.

This teaching will be powerful and effective when it is given to an individual who has done a great amount of inner work, and who has developed his awareness and his state of consciousness to a very subtle and high level. When the individual reaches the state of inner development where it is possible to see personally the issue of desire, the teaching can then act. But even then, it is not enough for the individual to be able to perceive the subtle movement of desire for him to be willing to let go of desire. He must also be at the stage where he sees and feels that desire is a nuisance, an obstacle. He must be able to see and feel that desire is an issue to be dealt with.

It is easier to understand this point if we consider something simpler than desire. Let's consider a person who is habitually critical and judgmental of other people. This person can be quite aware of his bent of mind. He can also be aware of how badly he feels when he is critical. But this does not necessarily mean he will stop. He might continue being critical in a very righteous way, regardless of his perception of the situation. He still does not see his criticalness as something undesirable. This is a very common situation.

The criticalness is seen as "ego-syntonic" for this individual; that is, it is in accord with his personality and does not feel alien or undesirable to him. It goes along with, and is part of, the person's conception of himself. It is not felt as disharmonious with his well-being. A trait, like criticalness, has to become "ego-alien" for a person to do something about it, or even to see it as an issue to be understood. "Ego-alien" means that it is experienced as being alien to the ego, as not consistent with the person's interests, as conflicting with the rest of him.

So no trait or part of the personality can become an object for understanding and dissolution as long as it is ego-syntonic. When it becomes ego-alien, then the person will become uncomfortable in such a way that he will be concerned about looking at this part of the personality and doing something about it.

Returning to the issue of desire, we see that desire does not become a focus for inner work until the individual sees it as ego-alien. For the average student, desire is experienced as ego-syntonic for a long time, and hence it is not seen as an issue. This is especially so for persons in the human community who have not chosen to follow the path of inner work. These people are very far from seeing desire as being ego-alien. In fact, desire is part of the fabric of everyday life for most of humanity.

No wonder then, that so few individuals respond to such teachings. To say to the average man that he must eradicate desire in order to be happy is absurd. For one thing, this has no meaning for him; but more importantly, desire is still ego-syntonic. The form that the teaching is presented in is experienced as ego-alien by most people. *The teaching itself is experienced as ego-alien.* It will have to be experienced as ego-syntonic for there to be a response. This means it will have to be presented in a way that is ego-syntonic. The teaching must take into account that the student must experience in his own life that desire is an obstacle, that it thwarts him in his purpose.

So the issue here is not just a matter of accuracy in stating the teaching. If the teaching is to be broadly and comprehensively effective, it must be presented in a way that is digestable to the average person, and digestable to the student. This is a matter of communication, of appropriateness, of tact, of skill, of understanding. The individual's mind and state of consciousness need to be taken into consideration for the communication to be appropriate and effective.

We have discussed the situation in very general terms, and only in regard to the teachings concerning desire, but our understanding has a much wider application. It applies to the more specific situations, and to other deep issues of the teachings.

In the relationship between teacher and student, it is the responsibility of the teacher to communicate appropriately and with tact. This is what makes a teacher a good and effective one. An effective teacher will handle a situation in a very personal way for the student, taking into consideration the unique situation of the student and his state of consciousness. He will see that the issue of desire, for instance, will have to wait until the time comes when the student is ready to understand desire. He will do what he can so that the student will eventually arrive at the stage where he will experience desire as ego-alien, as disharmonious with his well-being.

But if the teacher keeps discoursing to all his students on the subject of desire, without regard to individual variations, obviously he will not be effective in his work with them. Only a few of them will be able to respond and benefit. And we ask, how is this the fault of the student?

What we are finding here is that the inner work is a very intimate and personal thing. General teachings, regardless of how deep and universal, do not work. The teaching will have to be

In present teaching, life situation of student or concern of student must be considered.

formulated and communicated in a way that will effect the particular student in the most intimate and personal manner. The teaching must speak to the student's heart. He has to be able to relate the teaching to his own life in a very personal way. He has to see that it deals with his everyday concerns and conflicts, specifically and deeply. Otherwise the teaching is not useful, is not effective.

There are teachers who do take into full consideration their students' state of consciousness and particular life situation. But they are rare, and most teachers, at least most well-known teachers, do not operate this way. They offer the general principles of the teaching without discrimination to all their students, and their systems have set principles and set practices which all students have to abide by, irrespective of their individual differences.

Individual concern with the student's situation must not be confused with a personal relationship with the student. The teacher might be paying personal attention to the student's suffering and progress, but he might still be dealing with the whole situation from the perspective of the general principles of the teaching. In other words, the teacher might well be very concerned about the particular student, but still be talking to him, and attempting to deal with him from a general perspective that is neither appropriate nor precise for the student's situation at that time. For instance, the teacher might be trying to focus the student on the issue of having or not having a self. And although the student's issue is certainly at the deepest level that of self or no-self, the student might be far more concerned and far more in conflict over the issue of having or not having value. The student might be so concerned about his lack of self-value that he cannot relate to the question of self. And as a result, the teacher might tell the student—albeit lovingly and compassionately—that he is too concerned with himself, that he is self-centered and that is why he is suffering.

Although this is true, the issue of self is still ego-syntonic. Regardless of how much the student loves and respects his teacher, he cannot make the issue of self his personal concern. He is concerned with the issue that he feels he has no value. He says, "I feel and believe that I have no true value." The teacher says, "You are too concerned with yourself. Maybe you need to disidentify with your sense of self." The student, although he might outwardly agree, will feel deep inside, "This guy is not talking to me. I am suffering because I feel worthless, I feel my self has no value. I need to deal with this before I can even think of having or not having a sense of self."

Both teacher and student are right, but they are communicating at different levels, and the teacher has not understood what is more crucial for the student to deal with at that time. The fact is that if the student deals with the issue of value, and understands it, he will be able to move from it, and eventually will see that the issue of self is at the root of it. He will arrive at this deeper level in his own time, but not until this other more urgent layer, value, has been recognized and worked through. We might tend to think that because he feels that his self has no value, it will be easier for him to let go of it. But the conditioning of the personality does not work that way. It is likely that if the individual feels a lack of value he will not let go of his attachment to self, because this is supposed to bring liberation and fulfillment, and he feels too worthless to deserve such an attainment.

We are seeing more and more that the teaching cannot be done in a general way. Universal teaching, regardless of how deep and true, must be tailored to the specific needs of the particular individual. Otherwise, the teaching will be ineffective, and it is no fault of the student.

A particular instance is very instructive here, that of the teachings of Krishnamurti. He has been teaching for about fifty years now about a certain understanding. His teaching is mainly that of centerless, egoless awareness. If a person just pays attention to the process of the mind, how it is self-centered, how it consists of knowledge that depends on time and memory, there will arise free awareness, empty of all self or ego, and this free, egoless awareness will bring an end to fear, conflict and suffering.

In his discourses, Krishnamurti brilliantly describes this aspect of reality, the aspect of emptiness-awareness. His elucidation of this way of experiencing reality is possibly the best there is. He is speaking of a very deep truth, one of the deepest possible for a human mind. It is a truth that actually points to a necessary condition of enlightenment and liberation. However, how effective has Krishnamurti been? Thousands and thousands listen to the truth of his discourses. His followers love him, can see and appreciate him as a free man, but how many understand this deep and universal teaching, and have attained the realization that Krishnamurti has attained? There is not one single instance known. Why is this? He embodies the state he speaks of. His teaching comes directly from his personal experience. Still, nobody understands completely. Nobody understands in a way that is real, a way that will make a difference, a permanent difference. He has been unable to communicate his perspective in its most important aspects.

There are people who do understand Krishnamurti fully, but these few already had this understanding through their own efforts, and were developed enough in their consciousness to be able to listen to him and comprehend him.

Krishnamurti's teaching, although it is simple, elegant and true, proves to be not relevant to most of the people who listen to him. They cannot understand him, because they need to understand many other things about themselves and their minds before they can even relate to what he says. His words do not penetrate them, his teaching does not relate to their personal lives. Many of them understand him intellectually, but that is not a real understanding, and they believe what he says, but it does not transform them.

Krishnamurti says his teaching is simple and direct. He has said that a person can listen to him and understand him, and be transformed right there, before leaving the lecture hall. This is all very true, but it is simple and direct only to Krishnamurti's own perception. The state he is describing is experienced as simple. It is simple, and ordinary, and very near to the individual. It is, in fact, the very nature of awareness: simple, empty, clear.

But his teaching does not take into account the state of consciousness of most of his listeners. Their minds are preoccupied with other things, are full of all kinds of concerns and conflicts that they are not about to give up. These concerns and conflicts make up not only their lives but their very identities. They cannot therefore just be simply aware.

Krishnamurti is in fact asking his listeners nothing less than to give up their ego and their sense of self identity. But there is a lot involved in this sense of self and much of it is unconscious, not available to awareness. It is the sense of self that still governs the mind, the movement of thoughts, the focus of attention.

Not only is it not easy for the listener to understand Krishnamurti, the average student cannot take Krishnamurti seriously. If the listener searches his mind and heart, he will most likely see that he is not concerned with what Krishnamurti talks about, that he does not see how it relates directly to his own experience. It is true that Krishnamurti talks about such things as fear, and these are concerns of everybody, but what he says about it is not in the realm of most people's experience. An individual can, at most, see that Krishnamurti makes sense, that his discourses are logical, but minds and hearts do not operate according to logic and common sense. Powerful forces operate in the depths of the mind, forces which must be understood first, or they will always prevent the individual from seeing the simple truth in Krishnamurti's teaching.

He might appreciate the simple and elegant truth of Krishnamurti's teaching, but his ego is usually not able to tolerate such simplicity. So, he ends up believing it only intellectually. The depths of his unconscious do not get touched. In fact, Krishnamurti's teaching is experienced by such an individual as alien to his best interests. This is true for most people if they are really honest with themselves. There is no reason for the listener to believe that the condition Krishnamurti talks about is desirable or that it will bring about his salvation. He outwardly agrees with Krishnamurti that emptiness and egoless awareness are wonderful, but inwardly he does not really know that. Buddha said the same thing about emptiness and passive awareness, so that tends to support Krishnamurti's discourses, but it does not really touch the listener's heart. There is nothing in the person's experience that will make him really and truly believe Krishnamurti. Emptiness and passive awareness—regardless of how many enlightened masters have attested to its power and freedom—are only words for the listener. At most, he can associate a vacuity with it. And why should he value this sense of vacuity or nothingness? No part of his experience tells him he should, so in his unconscious he rejects emptiness regardless of how much he believes in it consciously. Krishnamurti's teaching about the necessity of understanding the search so that the search will end, is cogent and useful. However, regardless of how much sense it makes to the mind of the listener, his heart most likely will not respond to such a teaching.

So why do people continue for many years following Krishnamurti, pursuing this state which he embodies and speaks about? The answer might be that there is in the students attracted to such a teacher, some inkling, some hint, of the state of clarity and pure awareness. Krishnamurti's discourses bring this clarity more strongly into his listener's presence. The student is seeking his own clarity, so to speak, and since Krishnamurti is clear, the student believes that Krishnamurti can show him the way to it. But as we have noted, nothing is done for or about the enormous baggage of mind, emotion, self-image, etc., which the student believes to be his identity. Furthermore, Krishnamurti's teaching is not merely about clarity, which is desirable to many. His concern is about *selfless* or *centerless* awareness, which is usually unfathomable to most of his listeners.

The individual first needs to have learned a great deal about life and about his own mind for him to come close to understanding or appreciating the simple and beautiful teachings of Krishnamurti. Krishnamurti's teachings will be useful and appropriate for the individual who has refined his consciousness to such a degree that he starts seeing his ego or sense of self as alien to his best interests. Then, and only then, will Krishnamurti's insights be instantly transformative.

Krishnamurti is talking about himself, his experience, his state, and is genuinely trying to communicate it to others. Although his experience is that of freedom, it is not close to most people's experience of themselves. Even though they can appreciate the words they hear, it will be difficult for them to relate to the actual experience itself. He is not taking into consideration his listeners' situations, their minds, their levels of development, and states of consciousness.

Krishnamurti's consistent personal experience is of emptiness and its pure awareness, its freedom and its truth. He has known it for most of his life. By now it is his mind. It is he, himself, so it is what he speaks. A master's teaching is always an expression of himself. If he embodies freedom, then he speaks of freedom. It is not that Krishnamurti does not listen to his students. It is not that he does not understand them. But let us say he understands them within the framework of his own experience, from his own perspective. And that perspective of his, a perspective of pure awareness, of emptiness, of freedom from the mind, is a perspective that most of his listeners cannot relate to.

As we have seen, a master speaking to a student from his own perspective is not enough for effective teaching. Much more is needed, much more must be taken into consideration. Some teachers do understand this, and attempt to take the student's individual situation into account. But even then it is difficult for a teacher to disengage from his own state of consciousness and to tailor his perspective to the needs of his student.

Bhagwan Rajneesh, for example, seems to understand Krishnamurti's predicament, and tries to take the levels of consciousness into consideration. He knows the state that Krishnamurti teaches, but he knows that most people cannot relate to it. So he gives many different practices, and different kinds of discourses relevant to the different personalities and the various states of consciousness, and in this way tries to remedy the situation we are discussing.

However, we observe here too it is difficult for him to disengage completely from his own state of consciousness. Although he discourses on all kinds of topics, his main emphasis is always the loss of ego boundaries or the loss of the sense of ego and its separateness. He connects all practices and all teachings ultimately to the state of ego death. In fact, all his discourses are delivered from the perspective of a certain state of consciousness, that of cosmic or divine consciousness. His title, itself, is "Bhagwan," "The Divine," and he is a beautiful embodiment of this divine state. So his teaching is a teaching of the state of egoless divine consciousness. All his discourses are imbued with this level of realization. This consciousness gives his discourses their beauty and their universality.

As we have mentioned, Rajneesh offers various practices in order to reach his audience. But we have also noticed that when he discourses it is his own personal state which dominates, his own personal state which is communicated. He cannot discourse without his own state being the one communicated. This is a situation all spiritual teachers face. We have mentioned Rajneesh as an example, to consider this difficulty. The fact that the teacher's state is wonderful and his teachings are beautiful, does not guarantee effectiveness and success. The student might need something else.

Ultimately, it is true, the student needs to arrive at this state of egoless cosmic consciousness, for this is a stage on the way to liberation. But, this state might be irrelevant for him at the time regardless of how beautiful it looks on his guru. The student might need to see and learn a state of solid will, for example, because he happens to be in need of resolving his issues, his life situations, that are centered around the aspect of will. It is true the individual will have to learn to let his ego boundaries dissolve and let go of his sense of individuality. But how can he let go of his sense of individuality until he knows he has one? First he will need to see that he has individuality; he has to see and understand what individuality is before he can let go of it. He also needs to see how his ideas about individuality and his holding onto them lead to suffering. He has to see that his sense of individuality and his attachment to his sense of self do not lead to fulfillment and are not syntonic to his harmony or peace of mind.

An individual who is working to achieve ego death will be stymied in his endeavors if he does not first see very clearly and very definitely what ego is. Ego boundaries will first have to become ego-alien. The fact that a student intellectually believes that he needs to lose his ego, does not mean that he does believe it in the depths of his heart. In the depths of his heart he does not understand why he needs to let go of ego boundaries. The issue does not seem relevant to his mind, to his heart, to his life situation. In fact, ego death is a meaningless thing unless a very high and refined level of inner realization is reached. Ego is not seen as the issue until the individual is close to the state of cosmic consciousness.

Rajneesh understands this when he says a person must develop an individuality before he can surrender it. In his discussion of the psychology of the esoteric, he speaks of seven levels of consciousness in what he calls the seven bodies. In this system, he sees the fifth level as that of crystallized individuality. This fifth body, which he calls the spiritual body, first needs to be developed. Then the issue of loss of ego becomes relevant to the individual. He also mentions that the most difficult stage to achieve is that of the fifth body, the spiritual individuality, and once this is achieved, the transition to cosmic consciousness is not difficult.

This means that most people first need to develop the fifth level before the state that Rajneesh embodies can be most effective and transformative. So the state the student needs to see and learn is that of the fifth body, and a teacher who can embody this state of consciousness and operate from it will be most effective, for this state will then be communicated to the students who require it. It will be the fulfillment of their exact personal need at the moment.

It is our assumption here that the development of certain capacities and virtues on the material, emotional, mental and essential levels is desirable, and perhaps necessary, for the individual who seeks to attain the enlightened state promised by the various teachings we are examining here. Examples of such qualities we have referred to in this discussion are value, strength and will.

Buddhist, Sufi and Christian teachings often enumerate qualities considered as desirable to embody—love, humility, truth, for example. Here of course the same problem we have been addressing again arises: the student cannot voluntarily choose at an arbitrary moment to manifest humility, for example, until it is appropriate for his development, and until pride is experienced as ego-alien. (This matter is more fully discussed in Chapter Three.)

To put the matter conversely, the lack of such qualities, capacities and virtues constitutes a barrier to a person's realization. This is because their presence is actually normal in an optimally developed person, and their absence is always felt (often unconsciously) as a deficiency. In virtually every case, then, a significant part of one's motivation for spiritual seeking is to fill those felt deficiencies. Thus a teacher who is able to support a student in developing the specific capacities he needs to confront both ordinary human and spiritual challenges on the path, will be more effective than one who perceives and teaches only from a more "sublime" perspective.

This leads us to an important principle: the effective teacher will concern himself not only with the personal situation of the student, but optimally will also be able to embody and manifest the exact consciousness needed at the time by the particular student. The student needs to contact the teachings of the state of consciousness that is the exact resolution for his situation at the time. If the student is at the time dealing with issues of strength and weakness, for example, it will be inappropriate to try to teach him about freedom from desire or about egoless awareness or even cosmic consciousness. The teaching will be alien to him and to his interests, and hence ineffective. He will see it as alien to his well-being. He will not see it as speaking to him in a way that is relevant to his particular situation.

Some systems of inner work have tried to deal with this difficulty. In the past few centuries, for instance, the Sufi order of Naqshbandis in the Middle East had connections with all other Sufi orders. They would send the student to the order or teacher most appropriate for the stage of development of that particular student. Then, when he had absorbed that aspect of the teaching, he would be sent elsewhere to learn other things he needed for his ultimate development and liberation. Another system which has utilized a similar method is that of Vajrayana Buddhism, in Tibet. In various disciplines there have always existed a few teachers who are developed enough to manifest whatever state of consciousness is needed by their students at any time. We will return to this point in the next chapter.

One thing we see here is that any teaching built around a particular method or even a particular state of consciousness is bound to be limited, and will be effective only for the people who happen to need that particular state of consciousness. No particular method or particular state of consciousness can be applied universally to all people. This point is rarely heeded by either students or teachers, and ignorance of it always leads to frustration and waste.

For an example, we can take the systems or teachings formulated around devotion and surrender. A disciple is asked to surrender to his guru or to God. Some people have a need, at a given state, to practice surrender and devotion, and thus can benefit from systems emphasizing surrender. But even then the teachings are not really efficient. This is because surrender is a state of consciousness that requires much understanding and much preparation. Not only that, surrender can become ego-syntonic at one time, and not at another. The individual who is learning to assert himself because he was always weak and submissive should nôt be expected to view surrender as something syntonic to his best interests. In fact, his problem is that he surrenders too easily, out of self-deficiency, in a superficial way which is neither true nor real. As Rajneesh has said, an individual first needs to have a sense of self that is precious and for which he worked long and hard before he can surrender it; otherwise, what is he going to surrender? If he has no self, then he cannot give anything, to guru or to God. And, if he has a weak sense of self, then his surrender is vacuous. He is not really surrendering. A weak ego cannot surrender; it can only submit.

Even if surrender is understood as surrender to experience, it is not realistic to ask a student to surrender, because for most people, surrender, which is felt as being without defenses, means getting hurt. As children, people had the capacity for surrendering to their experience. Their hearts were open. But that openness did not bring about fullness and pleasure. The child, without defenses, was repeatedly hurt in that openness. Therefore openness of heart and surrender of defenses are usually equated in the unconscious with vulnerability, and this brings up the memory and fears of deep hurt. These fears, these associations with surrender, need to be understood and resolved before the individual can experience surrender as syntonic; otherwise surrender is seen as threatening, as contrary to what is best for him.

It is an unskillful tactic for a teacher to insist that a student surrender. The student may then try to surrender—but he is simply submitting to a superego demand. A more useful and compassionate approach is to help the student understand his fear of surrender and his resistance to it.

Also, when a student is expected to surrender to God or to reality, the question arises, why should he do this? He does not know what God or reality is. He hears that it is good and wonderful. His guru tells him that surrendering will bring about the experience of pure love and benevolence, but he has no personal knowledge of this. What he does know through personal experience is that surrender means pain.

He must first have some experience of surrender, and some exposure to sublime reality, before he can trust enough to let go of what is actually keeping him from this reality. When he has some taste, some experience of this reality, then surrender will become syntonic to his own aspirations. When he sees and tastes the love, beauty, and the grandeur of reality, then he cannot but surrender. At the very least, he will long to surrender.

A teacher who expects his students to surrender without regard to their personal situation, without helping them deal with their conflicts around surrender, is like a priest who expounds on selfless brotherly love to his assembly and then expects his listeners to behave from that perspective, and is disappointed if they do not. A Christian might consciously believe in the value of Christ-love, but he really has no experience, not even the vaguest idea, of what this means. He cannot act on it because he does not know what it is.

Most Christians have no experiential basis for believing in selfless love. Why should they be selfless? They do not know, do not understand why this is a good thing. Such a Christian's mind and heart neither understand nor believe in selfless love. He does not believe it because he has no personal evidence that it is desirable. He cannot see that selflessness leads to freedom. Instead he sees selflessness as loss, loss of what he cherishes and desires.

There is much talk about selfless love, selfless giving, selfless existence and so on. But the majority of human kind does not know what "selfless" means, let alone that it might be a beneficial state.

Since most people do not even know what it means to have a self, how can they know what it is to be selfless? So, when we preach selfless love, we are not communicating to most people. We are not taking into account how they think and live. This is inconsiderate, for to them, selfless love and selfless existence are quite alien, both in their minds and their experience.

The development and realization of selfless love, of Christ-consciousness, will liberate the individual, will bring about fulfillment. Christ's understanding of human suffering is very deep and true; his solution is universal. But it is not an easy thing to understand, to learn or to embody. Many things have to be learned first. Many things have to be developed in the soul before Christ-consciousness becomes possible to see. And then more inner work and refinement is needed before selfless love arises.

The issue of self or no-self does not become a personal issue for the student until he is near the end of his inner development and spiritual growth. Before that point, the question of self and no-self will be experienced as irrelevant.

Buddha saw that many people around him were very conscious and highly developed spiritually, but were still suffering; their realization had not freed them completely. He saw this for himself too. And only at this point did the issue of self or no-self become important to him. Solving this issue was his final accomplishment, the acme of his realization and his contribution to humanity.

This illustration demonstrates that for a teaching to demand selflessness of the beginning or even intermediate student is ridiculous, or at best, ineffective.

So we reach our final understanding, that some important factors contributing to the problem of effective spiritual teaching are those of communication, appropriateness, and most importantly, the fit of teaching and student. In general, we see that neither the average individual in the world nor the student on a chosen path is generally addressed by spiritual teachings in ways that make sense to them. Their minds, their situations and their states of consciousness are almost never taken into consideration. They are presented with teachings that they can only see as alien to their experience, as contrary to their well-being. So even the seeking student cannot really make the teachings his personal concern, because he does not see how they relate to him or to his life. And the average person can see no reason to look more deeply into the teachings.

If we do not make the teaching our own, if we cannot apply it to our lives, then the teaching cannot work for us, regardless of how deep, true or sublime it is.

CHAPTER THREE
THE SOLUTION

t would be difficult for us to find a satisfactory solution for our predicament if we restrict ourselves to the commonly accepted domains of experience, the realm of the mind and the realm of the emotions. We must extend our perceptions to the finer and deeper capacities that are locked within humanity. We must go deeper, to the realm of being, to our true essential nature, with its fine but unexpected capacities for perception and action.

From our analysis so far, we can see what is needed is for the teaching to be presented in a way that is appropriate to each particular individual. The teaching must be communicated to the student in a manner that is experienced by the student as syntonic to his experience. It will be introduced to him in a way that he can relate to and which has validity for him. The teaching will speak to him, to his experience. It will deal with his life as he lives it. It will help him deal with his own conflicts and issues, not those of Buddha or Krishnamurti.

The teaching will be formulated in a way that his mind can understand, and his heart can accept. It will be represented in a way that allows him to make it his own personal concern. It will speak to him from the perspective that he needs at the moment of contact. Then it will touch him. Then he can embrace it. Then he can use it. Then it can transform him.

Many a time a teacher will tell his disciple, "You need to jump into the abyss. You need to trust and jump." But for the disciple, what the teacher is saying has no meaning. The disciple, if he is allowed to be sincere, will most likely respond: "What do you mean, 'Jump into the abyss?' What abyss? Where is this abyss I'm supposed to jump into? Also, who or what is supposed to jump?" For the disciple this is a real dilemma, and it is not just a matter of trust.

The fact is that there is an abyss. It can be seen and felt. There is an individual who can jump. This individual can be identified in a very specific way. So the teacher will first have to work with his disciple on issues of identity. Then the teacher should guide the disciple to the place where the disciple can actually see or feel the abyss within himself. And only at this point will the teacher be effective in saying, "Trust and jump into the abyss." Only then is it an issue of trust. Before that, the student can only balk, or look at his teacher's statements as some kind of mysterious, mystical allusion that he is supposed to follow.

There is no place here for mystery and mystification. Mystification usually indicates the absence of true knowledge and understanding.

A teacher who can speak to a student in such an appropriate, tactful and timed way, is able to take into consideration the person of the student, his mind, his state of consciousness and his present-time situation. The universal and timeless teaching will be focused, narrowed down to a personal level at a point of space and time. Otherwise it is too abstract and lacks personal meaning for the student.

This personal focusing of the universal and timeless teaching begins with recognizing the student as a unique individual with his own experience, his own history, his own issues, and his own will, and not simply as an object upon which a teaching can be applied.

In most spiritual teachings, the personality is seen as a barrier, the problem, the devil that needs to be slain. Only then, it is believed, can realization occur.

It is true that a seeker's personality or his history is a large part of his problem, but it is so only from the perspective of a consciousness that he still cannot relate to. According to his own perception, the experiences of the personality are real, solid, and of great import. Rejecting or ignoring the personality will only tighten the knots that imprison the student.

Also, the issues and the conflicts of the personality are not haphazard or meaningless; they are not simply barriers to realization and liberation. They are related in specific ways to the states of realization themselves, to the states of being.

To gain a more precise understanding of the situation, and to personalize the teaching, we need first to understand the personality and how it is related to the free reality, the being—what we call essence. Our true nature, our essence, what is real and unconditioned in the human being, does not exist in some mysterious realm, waiting for us to attack and slay the inimical ego, and then show up in glory. Our being, our essence, the divine within us, is connected to our personality in a very complex and intimate way.

Before we discuss this connection, we must see that essence exists in many and various aspects, in pure and real forms. Each aspect is distinct from all other aspects, but it is still essence, it is still the same nature. For example, essence can manifest as love, but it can also manifest as compassion, and as will, peace, strength, consciousness, truth, contentment, knowledge, joy. The aspects of essence are differentiated, are distinct. Each is a pure form of itself. The aspect of truth is completely truth; it contains nothing that is not true. Each aspect is perfection itself.

The realization of these "qualified" aspects of essence is very useful in moving toward the realm of unqualified, undifferentiated Being, the Supreme aspect or form. But these aspects of reality are not within the realm of the intellect or the emotions, and that is why, as we mentioned before, we must go deeper to find a solution for our dilemma. We will find that the solution is much more accessible and more beautiful than we expected.

It is true that the personality as a whole acts as a barrier to essence as a whole. But this is the general picture. Although most teachings adhere to this picture, if we look more closely, with finer lenses, so to speak, we find that this is a blurred picture of a more complex reality.

We find that each of the essential aspects—such as will, love, truth, compassion—is related to a certain part of the personality, to a definite sector. We will also find that each aspect of essence is not only related to a certain sector of the personality, but also that that sector functions as a specific barrier against the particular aspect of essence in question. So, a certain sector of the personality which consists of specific beliefs, habits and conflicts will act as a barrier against emptiness, for instance. A different sector will act as a barrier against cosmic consciousness, and so on.

Each sector of the personality manifests as certain conflicts, issues, difficulties, prejudices, traits, preferences, and so on. These will be reflected in the individual's personal experience, both inner and outer. It determines, among other things, thoughts, feelings, actions, relationships, and life-styles.

We call this perspective on reality, on both essence and personality, the "diamond perspective." We call it such because it is exact, precise and definite, and it takes the many facets, the details, of both essence and personality into consideration. The elegance and beauty of its workings will become apparent as we go on in our discussion.

Now we go back to our human dilemma, and see how we can use this diamond perspective to find an effective solution.

Any individual, at any time in his life has a certain set of personal preoccupations and concerns which are manifestations of specific sectors of his personality. These are not haphazard. He is dealing with a specific set of issues, conflicts and life situations, and these might be quite different from those of other individuals in his environment. One sector of the personality might dominate his life for long periods of time if he is not successful in resolving the issues and conflicts inherent in it, and so it might appear to others, or to himself, that this is who he really is, this person acting out of this particular set of issues, that there are no other parts of him. The average individual moves between a few sectors of his personality, and most of these sectors are deeply hidden in his unconscious.

According to the diamond perspective, the sector of the personality that happens to be dominant at any given time is related to a certain and specific aspect of essence. In fact, according to the diamond perspective, the real resolution of the conflicts and issues in such sectors will bring about the manifestation of the related specific aspect of essence. The application of the diamond perspective which is set forth in more detail in our forthcoming book Essence (to be published by Samuel Weiser, Inc., in 1984), has demonstrated that the resolution of any particular sector, issue or conflict of the personality is actually the related essential aspect itself.

For an example, let us look at the sector related to the aspect of will, and so at the individual who has conflicts around castration, impotence, confidence in himself, self-reliance, need for support, and the like. Such conflicts and psychological issues govern his relationship to others, his actions in his life and his feelings about himself.

If he manages to resolve these personal issues, he will come in contact with his true and essential will. Then the manifestation of the aspect of will in him will spontaneously eliminate all these conflicts. He will experience a sense of true determination; he will feel confident in himself; he will feel self-reliant, potent, powerful and able to support himself in the way he needs. He will, most importantly, experience his essence directly in the aspect of will. He will not feel he *has* will, he will feel he *is* will—he *is* the support.

Now suppose this individual is the disciple of a teaching which emphasizes surrender, and he is feeling impotent and dependent. He is having problems with the sector of his personality corresponding to the aspect of will; he lacks will. He goes to his teacher or guru for help. The teacher being true to his teachings, advises the disciple that he needs to surrender to God's will. He needs to let go of his worldly concerns, of his personality. The teacher tells the disciple that he needs to be in touch with the aspect of his essence having to do with surrender—the part of his being in which his heart melts.

Now what will the disciple do? His need is not for the aspect of surrender. His exact need at the moment is for the aspect of will. His life, his situation, his mind, his heart, are all crying out for confidence and determination. But his teacher tells him he needs surrender. He loves his teacher. He trusts him. He believes him. But what can he do?

Here in a nutshell, we see the dilemma. No wonder nothing happens. The disciple goes back to his chanting or his prayers or his supplications. But obviously nothing happens, except frustration and more suffering. The teacher looks at his disciple, sees him doing his prayers, but can also discern under the surface that he is fighting, trying to assert his will. The teacher tells his student he is only pretending, that he is not really surrendering, not trusting.

It is true that the disciple is only pretending. But he is in a bind. His essence is approaching his consciousness with the aspect of will. Yet his guru—who is supposed to be the representative of essence— exhorts him to surrender. The teacher has his heart open, feels surrendered to God, and truly believes his disciple needs the same thing, needs to surrender his will.

It is true the disciple needs to surrender his will, or more accurately, attune it with reality. But first he must *have* his will. First he must resolve his personality issues that have to do with feeling castrated and weak. Then it is possible for him to surrender his will. So of course, unconsciously, he is looking for his will; he certainly is not surrendering, and his teacher is aware of this. However, although his teacher is right in his judgment, he is not right in the way he handles his student. He is making inappropriate demands, being blind to what the student requires specifically at the moment; he is being inefficient.

Some might object by saying that the student should surrender to God's will. God's will is will and since he needs will, then surrendering to God's will should resolve his conflicts.

But personal will and the Divine will are two distinct aspects of essence at the beginning. First, the individual needs to realize his personal will which is an actual, pure aspect of essence. Only then can he surrender or align his personal will to the divine will. Until then, he has no will to surrender.

Now, if the teacher happens to be oriented towards will, like Gurdjieff, then the student will be in good hands. Gurdjieff will know exactly what the student needs. Gurdjieff has will, embodies will, *is* will. So not only does he say the right words to the student, but the student can actually see and feel what will is like, for he sees it in the person of his teacher. This situation is exactly tailored for his personal needs. The teacher diagnoses accurately the problem of the student, and gives him the right teaching and the appropriate practices to deal with his situation.

The student can relate to the teaching. His heart is touched. The teaching is appropriate. It actually speaks to him. The teacher recognizes his personal concerns, his everyday occupations. His teaching addresses his personal present-day sufferings.

In addition, his teacher presents him with the resolution for his situation. The solution is right there in the person of the teacher himself: what he says, how he says it, how he moves, his voice, his posture—all these things emanate and express will—exactly what he needs.

The powerful presence of the teacher in the aspect of will ignites the student's approaching will, supports it and enhances it, pulls it out nearer to consciousness. There is a meeting between the student's consciousness and the teacher's consciousness. There is an implicit understanding, a merging, a union that transforms the student. Now he has will. Now he knows will. Now he is will. He feels solid, immovable. He feels there is solid ground beneath him, supporting him. He is this solidity. Not only that, he knows his essence—for will is an aspect of his essence, his true nature. This will be a tremendous help in actualizing the other aspects of his essence in all of its immensity.

Let us now suppose that the student is not dealing with issues related to will, but that his life is primarily dominated by issues of surrender. He feels strong, willful, rigid. His heart is hard. He is always guarding his independence and autonomy. He cannot surrender to feelings of vulnerability. He cannot love. In sexual relationships he cannot risk the openness of genuine intimacy; he cannot allow a sense of melting with his partner. He feels the lack of softness, or surrender. He is tired of being the strong one who never falters. He wants to give himself, but he cannot; he is afraid of losing his strength, his will, his independence, his individuality.

In this instance, Gurdjieff would be of no help. Gurdjieff and his system are will-oriented. Gurdjieff's teachings would not be appropriate. Performing super-efforts would just add to his rigidity, and lack of softness.

But the teacher who embodies the aspect of surrender would be effective with this student. Somebody like Ramakrishna, like Rumi, or a Hassid would be just right. Then not only will he receive the appropriate teaching for him, but he will also be in intimate contact with the quality of surrender itself. What is offered is exactly what he needs. He will be able to understand his issues, resolve his conflicts, and his heart will melt in the golden essence of love and surrender.

The aspect of surrender can help the person surrender to other aspects of essence. This will depend on the teacher again, and on the system of teaching, because if the system does not admit to the existence of other aspects, then the system itself will become a barrier against these aspects.

So the question arises: When a student is able to embody one essential aspect, such as surrender, what happens to the other aspects of essence? What happens to the other sectors of the personality?

This will depend on the student and the teacher alike. Normally, after one issue is dealt with, another sector of the personality is activated and starts dominating the individual's life. The order in which these sectors rise to consciousness is not predictable. What sector does arise will depend on the individual's personality and his present circumstances.

An individual who has just resolved his issues of merging and surrender, and has realized his essence in this aspect, might find himself beginning to feel weak. Issues relating to the aspect of strength have started to surface; he now experiences emotional conflicts around weakness and the desire for strength. He starts having doubts as to whether he is strong enough to separate from his past, or his dependency on his mother, or from his personality. He feels he has no energy to do anything. His pelvis is tight. He lacks sexual energy. He can merge with his love partner, but has difficulty consummating the sexual act. He needs strength, fire, energy, expansion. But whenever he feels strong, he also feels angry; he cannot differentiate between strength on the one hand, and anger and hostility on the other.

In this particular case, strength is approaching—this is known as the fire aspect of essence—and is pushing to the surface the issues that have kept it buried.

Again, the situation depends upon the teacher. If the teacher who is embodying and manifesting the golden aspect of surrender is able also to embody the aspect of strength, then the student is again in good hands. The teacher will be able to see and understand the new situation of the student. He will talk to him from the perspective of strength now, and not from the perspective of surrender. He will be able to shift spontaneously his manifestation to that of strength. He will give his student the teaching from the perspective of strength, energy and expansion. He will be able to talk to him in a personal way about his most intimate feelings and conflicts. He will give the student practices that deal with his particular situation and ignite his fire and strength.

The teacher will shift his own state of consciousness; his presence will now be strength. He embodies strength. His words, his gestures, his stories, his posture, his actions—all emanate strength, energy, vitality. His presence is expansive. His ideas are sweeping and bold. He is alive, full of vitality and vigor. His fire-like quality beckons the strength of the student, sparks it, brings it forth. He sets his student's presence ablaze with his own magnificent expansion. Fire unites with fire. There is a union, a union that consumes the student's conflicts about strength as the essential aspect of strength frees him. It ignites his passion. His spirit is now passionately in the service of essence.

If, however, the teacher is not aware of the necessity to communicate this aspect of strength, he will not embody it. If the individual is still directed toward surrender, even his issues about strength will be seen by the system from the perspective of surrender. Either the student's efforts will be stymied, and he will be left with frustration and suffering, or his personality will start to stabilize around the aspect of essence already realized—the merging aspect of surrender. This latter phenomenon is rare, although it can happen, depending, among other factors, on the student and his personality structure. The discipline of the system based on surrender is usually structured around enhancing and developing the merging golden aspect of essence. In rare instances, the discipline and the related practices can succeed in crystallizing the consciousness of the student around this aspect.

But the best course for the student is to deal with his arising conflicts around strength, in order to realize this aspect of essence. He can of course go to another teacher, like Sai Baba, who embodies the aspect of strength. But it is important to understand that the student himself is seldom aware of his exact needs. He is not even aware that there is such a reality as that of the strength aspect. And this is why it is crucial that the teacher be alert and able to embody the aspects of essence that are specifically required by the student for the resolution of his issues, in whatever order they may appear.

As we described earlier, some schools like the Naqshbandi Sufi order will send the student to the teacher of one Sufi order and then to another and then to another. By working with teachers who embody specific aspects of essence, the student is able to resolve various sectors of his personality, and actualize the corresponding aspects of essence in himself. This process can continue until the personality is clarified and the student can let go of his ego-identification, to experience the cosmic aspect of essence, the freedom aspect of essence, and the various other aspects without the centeredness of the ego.

It is becoming obvious in this discussion that the ideal situation for the seeker is to be in contact with the right teaching at the right time, so that each sector of the personality is resolved as its corresponding essential aspect is realized. However, this is not possible for the individual to do on his own, except in the rarest of instances. Our concern here is more with the effectiveness of the teachings for the greatest number of people. Also, there are very few schools like the Naqshbandi, who implement something like the diamond perspective by sending students to different teachers.

Of course, the most effective teaching will be a complete teaching, a teaching that is cognizant of all aspects and has the understanding of each single aspect. The more aspects of essence a teacher understands and embodies, the more effective he is. The most effective teacher, the teacher who can reach the greatest number of individuals, is obviously the one who understands and embodies all aspects of essence. He can perceive the situation of any student, can give the teaching appropriate to the student at each stage of his development, and can manifest each of the aspects as they are needed by the particular student.

This kind of teacher, the complete teacher, is a realizable ideal. There are accounts of teachers like this who can reach the various kinds of personalities, and can guide a disciple through all the stages. Buddha is known to have possessed this capacity. He refused to expound on metaphysical questions and restricted his discourses and teachings to the needs of the particular student. Mohammed is known to have said: "Talk to each individual according to his capacity for understanding."

Many people involved in the paths of inner realization believe that if any teacher is realized or enlightened then he can understand every student. This is not true. Almost all teachers are specialized in one or more aspects of essential reality. Such teachers can at best understand all students from the teacher's own perspective. The teacher centered in cosmic consciousness can understand all students, but he can understand them only from the perspective of his own state—that of cosmic consciousness. His understanding is accurate, but as we have already shown, it might not be the kind of understanding most effective for the student.

Understanding the student from the perspective of the essential aspect that he happens to be dealing with is far more effective for him than any other kind of understanding. This is because it will speak to him directly in a most immediate and personal way, and only the complete teacher, one who has resolved all the sectors of his personality and who can embody any aspect of essence whenever it is needed, will be able to understand each student from the perspective that is most useful to him.

The Indian teacher, Sri Aurobindo, understood this point clearly. He writes that the person operating from the enlightened state like that of cosmic consciousness will be able to understand all points of view, but only by uniting them in one point of view—that of cosmic consciousness. But, he writes, this is not as powerful as understanding each point of view on its own. He speaks of his work as actualizing what he called the "supermind" which is a dimension of essential realization, a consciousness that is able to hold all points of view, all at the same time, and all equivalently.

The "diamond consciousness," responsible for the diamond perspective, is like Aurobindo's "supermind" in its capacity to look through all facets. Cosmic consciousness looks without facets so it sees everything, all points of view integrated in one perspective. The diamond consciousness can see all points of view, including the integrated point of view of cosmic consciousness, and hold all these perspectives and as equally valid.

An objection might be raised here that using one enlightened point of view, using one aspect of essence, can lead all the way to liberation from suffering, and that there is no need to use all aspects. This is quite true, and most realized individuals have become realized in this way. But we are concerned with the question of effectiveness, of a way of working that can be more effective for more people. Although it is possible to bring an end to personal suffering by using only one aspect, or perspective—such as awareness, or will, or surrender—it is at best, uncertain that this will occur. The rate of success of this approach is quite meager, as history attests. Most teachings have utilized one or a few aspects in their practices. If this approach were truly effective, we would see more success, we would see many more realized and liberated individuals. We started this book by seeing how ineffective most teaching systems are.

We can take a specific, well-known aspect, as an example to understand this point. This aspect of essence is that of energy. This is the pure self-existing energy that is usually called Kundalini or Shakti. Many teaching systems, many teachers, utilize this energy to accomplish total liberation. This approach certainly works sometimes, as attested to by the liberated individuals who have used this aspect of Kundalini.

However, we ask: How many people who use Kundalini do get liberated? Very, very few. And Kundalini is one of the most effective aspects when used on its own. Also, it is one of the easiest to activate.

The fact is that many people do get their Kundalini activated, but very few of them are able to use it to liberate themselves, even with the help of a realized master. The activation of Kundalini is not the same as liberation, and is not even a guarantee for it. The activation of Kundalini often only leads to more problems, more suffering, more stuckness.

A very strict discipline, a consistent practice, and preferably guidance by a very skilled and realized guide, are necessary for Kundalini to be used effectively. Even with all of this, the rate of success remains minimal. This is because Kundalini, like any other essential aspect, deals only with one sector of the personality and not with the whole thing. For Kundalini to bring about liberation, not only must the teacher be quite powerful, the disciple's dedication and discipline must be impeccable.

We can see this clearly and touchingly in the case of Muktananda in his spiritual biography. He belongs to a powerful and well-established lineage, the Indian Siddha path. His teacher, the Siddha master Nityananda, is powerful, firm, even severe with him sometimes. He keeps actualizing and strengthening Muktananda's Kundalini through his own Shakti, or spiritual power. But what we also see in the biography is Muktananda's impeccable patience, his consistent perseverance, his complete dedication to his *sadhana* (practice), his deep, unfaltering devotion to his Guru and his unwavering discipline. Not only that, he also lived a life of renunciation, celibacy and seclusion. Slowly, and with many pitfalls, with the guidance of his Guru, he was able to ascend to higher levels of consciousness, to the "blue pearl," and then to cosmic consciousness. His biography indicates that his Kundalini and other aspects of his work activated in him four primary, essential aspects— what he calls the Red Aura, the White Flame, the Black Light, and the Blue Consciousness.

But Muktananda is an isolated instance, a rare instance. How many others of Nityananda's students were realized like Muktananda? And how many of Muktananda's thousands of disciples have been liberated? He worked diligently all the time, imparting Shakti to his disciples, guiding them, and inspiring them. Many have their Kundalini activated; many have their hearts opened. But liberation still eludes them. They still keep moving in their personality cycles, hoping and waiting for the magical moment. It is not their fault, neither is it the fault of their Guru. The basic human dilemma of the persistence of suffering is operative here as it is in most situations.

It is a specific characteristic of Kundalini that it gives the individual an amazing amount of energy, without giving any understanding or wisdom. In the right context, it can lead to wisdom, but on its own it does not impart understanding. It does not resolve the individual's personal issues and conflicts. Its manifestation can lead to ego-death and cosmic consciousness, and then the essence can descend. But if we were to depend on Kundalini, the human dilemma would stay the same, and this does not offer much hope for many people.

However, there is hope. There is a unique and beautiful solution: namely, using essence itself to bring about the transformation. This does not mean that there is no need for deep work, dedication and devotion. All these are still necessary, but there is in essence a bigger help and a more accurate guidance.

We just said that Kundalini is an aspect of essence. This is true, but in a very specific way—in the sense that Kundalini is a true energy, the energy of essence. However, Kundalini is usually not seen as an aspect of essence because it is energy. Essence, in the strict sense of the word, is our being. It is the very substance of existence. Essential aspects exist on the being level and not on the energy level.

(Kundalini is usually known as the ascending force, distinguishing it from the descending force. The descending force through which people like Aurobindo attained their realization, is nothing but essence itself.)

Now, if there were a way to activate essence in such a way that it would keep manifesting one aspect after the other without being interrupted, then our solution would be found. And in fact, there is a way that will do just that. This has to do with a certain essential aspect, that of space—space, the dimension of emptiness, the dimension of the void. If a person can experience space, then essence will manifest spontaneously, one aspect following another.

The aspect of space is, just like any other essential aspect, related to a certain sector of the personality. Dealing with this sector, which has to do with self-image, will easily precipitate the experience of space. This in turn will activate the descending force, essence, in its various aspects. The presence of precise knowledge about this aspect of space, along with the presence of the teacher who embodies it or who embodies all aspects, will lead easily and quickly to the realization of this basic openness. This is because the issues concerning it, those connected to self-image, are usually close to the surface consciousness of the individual. Most people deal with self-image most of the time, and its issues are thus more available to consciousness than the other sectors of the personality.

When the openness of space is realized, it has an allowing influence on the other aspects of essence. Space becomes the emptiness that can be filled by any aspect of essence. Very shortly an essential aspect starts approaching consciousness, or descending into consciousness as some prefer to say. But as we have seen, in the diamond perspective, each aspect is connected to, and actively resisted by, a certain sector of the personality. This sector of the personality surfaces to consciousness and a particular set of conflicts and issues starts to dominate the individual's consciousness. Questions that were not his concern before, now become most intimate personal concerns; they become burning questions.

This great service which essence performs for us is difficult to appreciate. Neither Kundalini nor any teaching, nor any teacher can do what essence can do. Essence makes us face parts of ourselves that we usually do not face, that we do not choose to face. When an aspect of essence begins to manifest, it changes our perception of the related sector of the personality from ego-syntonic to ego-alien. Sectors of the personality that were never questioned before, start being experienced as an imbalance in our equilibrium, as suffering or causing suffering.

As an aspect of essence pushes forward toward consciousness, it acts on the personality. Essence is a force, and the sector of the personality related to the emerging aspect of essence becomes stronger and more forceful in order to be able to resist the emerging essence and to keep it out of consciousness. The very existence of the personality depends on unconsciousness, on maintaining its established patterns and conditioning. The personality does not want to change. As essence emerges, the conflict between essence and personality will be magnified and become more obvious. The conflict between the unconditioned part and the conditioned part becomes the focus of attention. The relevant sector of the personality will manifest more and more strongly now in consciousness, until it becomes imperative for us to look at it and deal with it in a real and effective way. It becomes necessary for us to understand and resolve the issues related to this part of the personality. To avoid or ignore the issues becomes more difficult than to face them.

Here, essence acts as a perfect teacher. It does not, like most systems of teaching, try to make us deal with sectors of the personality that we personally experience as syntonic to our well-being. It actually disrupts our habitual equilibrium. Forcefully but gently, and in a balanced way, it reveals each sector of the personality as alien and contradictory to our best interests. No human teacher can be so exact, so effective, and so appropriate.

If the aspect of essence approaching consciousness is that of samadhi, for instance, it will push out the issues around desire. The individual will start seeing in his own experience how desire leads to suffering. He cannot help but experience the nature of desire, its movements, its action. He will see it not according to what the Buddha or Krishnamurti say, but according to his own experience. He will become forced to experience attachment to desire as contrary to the harmony and peace of his mind. It will become necessary for him to understand his desires. He will long, personally and deeply, for the desireless state. This will happen even if he has never heard any teaching about desire, even if he has never conceived of a desireless state.

This longing, this personal and intimate yearning for the desireless state, is the longing for the essential aspect of samadhi. As it pushes forward to consciousness, it not only exposes the issues, it also brings to consciousness the awareness of the lack of peace and the quietness of mind of the state of non-desiring. This awareness of deficiency, this hole in the being, this lack of the complete peace of mind of the desireless state of samadhi, makes the person long for this essential aspect, even if he doesn't know that there is such an aspect.

What a teacher essence is! It exposes the issues, makes us look at them as dystonic, makes us feel the lack of the essential aspect, makes us long for the aspect. Now the teaching about desire becomes our personal concern. It is no more only Buddha's concern, it is now our own personal concern; and it is such a burning issue for us, such a burning question that it makes us ache and long for an answer, a solution. We cannot rest. The nearness of essence does not let us rest until we find the answer, until we come to the solution.

Essence is even more magical and more beautiful than that. It does much more than expose and burn the personality. As it approaches consciousness, we start getting intuitive understanding about our situation, about our dilemma. As our consciousness is touched by the emerging aspect, essence infuses it with its quality, with its knowledge, with its teaching, with its understanding. Slowly, we start getting the teaching regarding desire, by ourselves, from our own essence. The understanding we get is completely relevant to our situation. It speaks to *us*; it resolves our personal conflicts. The understanding is lived, is alive.

As the desireless aspect of essence begins to emerge, it infuses our consciousness. The understanding of our suffering and our conflicts around desire coincides with the emerging of essence in consciousness. The intuitive understanding about desire dissolves the related sector of the personality. And as this part of the personality is burned away in the knowledge emanating from the essential aspect, the essence is then free to emerge. Now we are not only infused by the desireless state of samadhi, we are the very state of desirelessness itself. The essential aspect becomes the consciousness, becomes our being and our presence. We now know what it is to be without desires because we are not only desireless, but we are desirelessness itself. We are now the essential aspect of samadhi, desireless, peaceful, rested, expanded and deep. No movement of desire. No movement of attachment. No holding to anything.

No human teacher can perform such service to a student. He can embody and manifest the desireless state, but essence allows us to taste desirelessness, fills us with the very substance and consciousness of the desireless state of samadhi. It manifests in us in the form of this aspect. It manifests this aspect in us as ourselves, as our very being. Now we truly know, because now we are what we know. We do not have to look at any teacher. We have the perfect teacher in our very own being.

An important point to understand here, a point not seen by many teaching systems, is that essence is always needed for the right understanding to arise. Most teachers assert that the mind first needs to understand and see its many ways of going about things, and then the mind will stop, and essence will manifest.

The interesting thing is that these teachers assert at the same time that the mind cannot free itself.

What we see in the examples we have given so far, is that the mind cannot reach the necessary understanding on its own. It is truly incapable of freeing itself.

Only the presence of essence enables the mind to see and understand. When the appropriate aspect of essence is present (although the individual might not be conscious of it), it infuses the consciousness with its own reality. Only then is the mind able to see. The reality to be understood must be there, and it has to touch the mind, for it to see and understand.

The understanding of such fundamental realities as desire-lessness or selflessness is actually the understanding of certain aspects of essence; when these aspects are not present, the mind is unable to understand. Understanding can at best be intellectual.

In fact, the central function of the teacher is that he be the embodiment of essence. Because he is essence, he can transmit it to the student who is receptive to him. Then the presence of essence in the student will bring about the transformation.

True, the mind must respond, must see and understand, for there to be a transformation. Otherwise it will block the force of essence. The mind does part of the work, but cannot do the whole work. The other half of the work, the more fundamental half, is done by essence itself, by its very presence. Essence is the transformative agent.

Essence is a relentless teacher. It does not stop at any aspect. After one aspect is understood and realized, it starts manifesting another aspect. This aspect in its turn now pushes into consciousness the particular sector of the personality connected to it, and makes it imperative for us to understand and resolve it. The emerging aspect makes us feel the lack of its quality. It makes us long and yearn for it. Gently but consistently, intelligently and knowingly, it puts pressure on us to start longing for it. Then it provides us with the insights, the intuitive knowledge that help us understand our disharmony. And finally it shows itself, culminating our experience by manifesting itself as a complete and absolute resolution for our conflicts.

Essence is then the teacher. Essence is then the taught. Essence is then the freedom. Essence is then the realization. Essence is then the fulfillment. Essence is then the being. Essence is then the very nature and substance of the individual. Essence is then the experience, the experienced and the experiencer. Essence is then the truth. Essence is then the nature of all reality.

This process of essential development continues as personality is clarified and worked through. Essence manifests itself to the individual's consciousness as the true strength, will, joy, compassion, love, peace, truth, fulfillment, consciousness, awareness, knowledge, freedom, samadhi—as one aspect follows another. The amazing richness of essence manifests in that there is an essential aspect for every important human situation or condition. The aspect that is experienced is experienced as the complete and exact fulfillment for these situations. The exactness, the precision and fitness are astounding. The beauty of essential action cannot but fill the consciousness with wonderment.

There is, for instance, an aspect that relates to pleasure, and this is different from the aspect of joy, which is different from the aspect of fulfillment, which is different from the aspect of satisfaction, and so on. There is the aspect of personal will, which is different from the universal or divine will. Then there is the aspect of essential conscience which guides one's life style and manner of relating to others. There are aspects that lead to the harmony of one's environment. There is an aspect that acts as a protector of the essential life which is different from the aspect of the defender of essence. There are aspects that relate to love and its various manifestations. There is a light, fluffy love, compassionate love, merging love, passionate love, divine love, and so on. The richness and the beauty of essence are endless. And the beautiful thing is that this richness acts at the same time to resolve personal conflicts and disharmonies.

The personality slowly loses its grip. The conditioning is gradually shaken loose, and the ego is exposed in its bankruptcy. Finally, the aspect of death manifests, and then the ego-identification starts dissolving. This marks the entrance into the divine realm of essence, where grace and mercy begin descending into consciousness, dissolving more and more of the ego boundaries. This ultimately leads to the understanding of enlightenment, and the emergence of the Supreme aspect. There is even an aspect that has to do with the search and with the end of seeking.

This in turn brings about the manifestation of the magnificence, the majesty, the exquisiteness, the magic, and the beauty of essence. Now, ego does not need to be slain. One does not have to wage war against ego, conquer or destroy it. Ego cannot but shatter at the recognition of the sheer beauty of essence and all of existence. It cannot but melt in the experience of the overwhelming precision and delicacy of essence. It cannot but bow and surrender at beholding the magnificence and majesty of reality.

Essence—the teacher, the tempter—becomes ultimately the very stuff of our consciousness, the very substance of our beingness, the beauty of all existence.

No wonder that essence is called the agent of inner transformation, the elixir of enlightenment. The elixir is the hope, it is the solution, and it is the fulfillment.

RIDHWAN

*A Work School dedicated to the discovery,
development, and preservation of the Human Essence.*

The source of our Work is the same as that of all genuine Schools of the Work of any time or place. In our School, however, we do the work of liberation using a new method. In this method we have integrated in a specific and precise way some of the ancient knowledge about the Human Essence and its development with the contemporary body of knowledge that shapes the present day mentality. In particular, we have studied, expanded, and fitted various aspects of knowledge and techniques from the major schools of psychology and psychotherapy, including the body approaches, to the work of liberation and realization. Our methods and techniques have, in effect, developed in the present environment, amidst the latest findings of the various psychological schools.

For more information, write:

Ridhwan School
P.O. Box 10114   or
Berkeley, CA 94709-5114

Ridhwan School
P.O. Box 18166
Boulder, CO 80308-8166